T3-BNY-865

Charles Faudree's Country French Living

Charles Faudree's Country French Living

Charles Faudree with M. J. Van Deventer

Photography by Jenifer Jordan

NEW HANOVER COUNTY
PUBLIC LIBRARY
201 CHESTNUT STREET
WILMINGTON, NC 28401

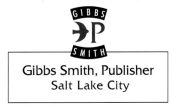

Gibbs Smith, Publisher
Salt Lake City

First Edition
09 08 07 06 05   10 9 8 7 6 5 4 3 2

Text © 2005 Charles Faudree
Photographs © 2005 Jenifer Jordan

All rights reserved. No part of this book may be repro-
duced by any means whatsoever without written permis-
sion from the publisher, except brief portions quoted
for purpose of review.

Published by
Gibbs Smith, Publisher
P.O. Box 667
Layton, Utah 84041

1.800.748.5439 orders
www.gibbs-smith.com

Designed by TTA Design
Printed and bound in Hong Kong
End papers: "Sintra" by Pierre Frey

Library of Congress Cataloging-in-Publication Data
Faudree, Charles.
  [Country French living]
  Charles Faudree's country French living / Charles
Faudree with M.J. Van Deventer ; photography by
Jenifer Jordan.— 1st ed.
      p. cm.
  ISBN 1-58685-715-0
  1. Faudree, Charles. 2. Interior decoration—United
States—History—20th century. 3. Decoration and
ornament, Rustic—France—Influence. I. Title:
Country French living. II. Van Deventer, M. J.
III. Jordan, Jenifer. IV. Title.
  NK2004.3.F378A4 2005
  747'.092—dc22
                                        2005018565

contents

table des matiéres

foreword

avant-propos

I'VE ALWAYS ADMIRED PEOPLE who have style, but I absolutely adore people who share their sense of style with others. Charles Faudree is the dean of this latter group of beloved individuals. By allowing editors like me to publish his design work in our magazines, Charles provides access to his unique and considerable talents for millions of Americans. I know from my fourteen years as editor in chief of *Traditional Home* the positive impact of this generosity is both instant and lasting.

And it often came in the form of reader mail! As soon as we released an issue that carried Charles Faudree–designed interiors, the letters would start to pile up in our mailbox. People who were new to the work of the prolific designer were wooed by the luxurious beauty he creates. They kept us busy for weeks answering intent questions about every fabric, finish, paint color, and item shown in our photographs. Readers who were already initiated to Charles' magic applauded our latest installment and often in their letters referred to their favorite rooms from past stories. Over the years, we became a clearinghouse for the Faudree fan club, and we loved every minute of it.

The effect of Charles' work is lasting; it delights the tenth time you see it almost as much as the first time. While I know many of his rooms by heart, I still stop to devour every detail when I meet them again on an occasional trip through past issues. Just as you know a Chopin sonata by the first few bars, you also know a Faudree room by the first few glances.

His perennial trademarks include classic upholstery chairs that beckon with beauty, fabrics that entice the eye and the touch, and antiques well loved and perfectly placed—all flavored with his signature French accent. The familiarity is endearing.

Charles is generous with his talents and also with his interiors. His favorite design principle, "too much is never enough," means every surface, detail and corner is considered. Nothing is overdone, but everything plays a role in each masterfully orchestrated scheme. There is abundance in his work. A dining table is accompanied not just with chairs but also a bench and maybe a settee. Miniature upholstered chairs are placed at the foot of the bed or snuggled up to a coffee table. Pillows come in triplets and are always stylishly turned out. Wooden chair frames are gracefully carved or embellished with color or gilt. The result is a seamless sonnet of a life that's well lived and also well appointed. Lucky for us, Charles shares this world of his in every one of his exquisite rooms.

If I could give any gift to him in return, it would be to always introduce Charles to more new friends. I hope this foreword fills some part of that wish and you'll pass along the favor to another in your circle. They'll thank you over and over again.

—KAROL DEWULF NICKELL
Editor in Chief, *Better Homes and Gardens*

My Favorite Things

mes préférées

IN 1978, AS I WAS ABOUT to turn forty, I gathered the courage to leave my sales position and move from Dallas, my home for many years. I wanted to pursue my dream—interior decorating—and chose to move back to my childhood home, Muskogee, Oklahoma, to open my first design studio and antiques shop.

Nancy E. Ingram discovered me there and published my very first house in *Tulsa Home & Garden* magazine, and Nancy and I have been together ever since. As she says, "We have had quite a trip together and we're still on the road." I am a decorator and I am proud to say that. I thank God every night for my talent and my wonderful clients.

Since that first story, my homes and those of my clients have been featured in almost every design magazine. But for years I wanted to do a book of my own. Jenifer Jordan, a great interior photographer, said, "I think I have a book in me, too, and I would love to do it with you." Nancy agreed.

Then M. J. Van Deventer signed on to help me write. We grew up together in Muskogee and she's interviewed me and written about my work for years. She has an amazing way of finishing my sentences for me. Our first book, *Charles Faudree's French Country Signature,* was released in October 2003 and is currently in its

eighth printing. Now, here we are again—our great team, including editor Madge Baird—with our second book. We hope you enjoy it as much as we have enjoyed producing it.

Through the all-new photography we introduce you to some of my favorite clients across the country and abroad. One of them is Joanne Hearst, who once owned a duplex next door to me in Tulsa. When she hired me to redecorate the duplex, she picked out the main fabric for each room and then went out of town and left everything else up to me, saying that she wanted it decorated down to the soap in the dish. It was absolutely the perfect job.

When Joanne returned to Tulsa after a seven-month absence, the duplex was done. She didn't call the next day or the next, and I was convinced she didn't like it. However, when she did call, she simply said, "I don't know where you have been all my life, but you're going to be with me the rest of my life." That was almost eight years ago, and we have been working on her seventy-five-year-old *finca* (farm) in Spain for the past four years. Her home—the manor house for a tiny village near Seville—is featured in this book.

People are always asking me where my favorite places are. Paris, of course, is my favorite European city and I go there at least once a year. If you have not been to the Paris Flea Market, let me tell you that it is truly a delightful experience. It is huge and each vendor rolls up his doors to a space no bigger than a one-car garage filled with seventeenth- and eighteenth-century furniture. Outside on the streets, other vendors tease shoppers with folding tables filled with junque. I love it all, and never tire of going there. Contrary to what you may have heard, I have never found the French to be rude, and the Paris Flea Market loves Americans.

I'm often asked if I speak French, and even though I am of French heritage, I don't speak the language. When I was sixty-five years old, I decided to take French lessons. After five lessons, we started learning about how a chair is female and a sofa is male, and I got out of there. That is not my kind of language. Plus, when I go to France, they don't even understand the few words I do know due to my Oklahoma twang, like *com bien* (how much)? I'm not much of a wheeler-dealer; it's easier for me to negotiate prices on paper, with my Bic pen in hand.

I love London almost as much as Paris, but for different reasons. There is no place like Paris, with its romantic language, wonderful food and wine. However, the English seem to understand "Okie" better, plus the English theater is so delightful. I go to England to buy what I call "smalls." The French don't have small accessories and I do love Staffordshire, Majolica and English tea boxes.

There are so many things I've collected in Paris and London that have become treasured possessions. My clients know I have sold some of my houses totally furnished, with certain exceptions. The blackamoor and the large cow tureen, which you will see featured on the dining table in my current home, are two of my favorite things. There is also a painting that Jimmy Steinmeyer, the world's best room renderer and a life-

long friend, did of my three King Charles Spaniels. In case of fire, I would get Nicholas out first, then the Steinmeyer painting and the tureen. I don't have to worry about the blackamoor anymore. My brother-in-law, Dale Gillman of Tulsa's Antique Warehouse, is anything but subtle. Every time he came to my house, he would remind me to be sure to leave the blackamoor to him. So I gifted it to him on his sixtieth birthday. I had enjoyed it for twenty-five years and figured it was his turn. I still get to see it because we live just across the way from each other.

The German Mateloch tureen has an interesting story. Although it is a favorite accessory, I didn't pick it out myself. On my fiftieth birthday, I was in London shopping with several friends on Portobello Road, which is a great flea market. They all chipped in and gave it to me as a present, and just for fun they filled it with boxes of instant chicken noodle soup.

My friends and clients know how much I love my blue-and-white collection. I started it right out of college and at that point only knew about Blue Willow. I have branched out since then and now collect English and Chinese export. This collection has been displayed at some point in every room, from the kitchen to the living room, in all of my homes.

Of course, Nicholas is a treasure. In this book, you will see him in almost every room of my house. He is not a prop, and I haven't trained him to perform. When we were photographing, we didn't move him from room to room, he's just a very loving companion who always likes to be wherever we are. Like many of your pets, he believes he is a person. And sometimes I'm not so sure he isn't.

Enjoy, with our team's best wishes.

—CHARLES FAUDREE

RUSSIAN FURNITURE
THE GOLDEN AGE 1780-1840   Antoine Chene

High Society

Southern Style

living spaces

les espaces à vivre

I BELIEVE THAT FIRST impressions are lasting so it is important to make entries welcoming and inviting. I like entries that provide a clue or a glimpse of what the rest of the house will look like. Whether it's a color theme, the style of furnishings, or a key to a homeowner's precious collections, it's nice to greet guests with that kind of welcome.

Several other rooms of one's home are also considered public areas—places where guests are welcome or entertained. Whether at formal parties or on spur-of-the moment occasions, people besides immediate family spend time in the living room, den or library, kitchen, dining room, and family room.

For me, the design of these rooms often begins with a pivotal fabric, a dominant color, or one magnificent antique. Just one distinctive piece of furniture, such as a towering armoire, an unusual commode, or a great accessory like a grand mirror or painting, will make the rest of the room seem more important. One outstanding piece can change the whole plan for a room. I encourage my clients to build their home around a few classic staples, just as you build a fashion wardrobe.

The fauteuil d' bureau *(desk chair) is a Louis XV/Louis XVI transitional piece that is home to one of my favorite needlepoint pillows, "Love me, Love my dog."*

I make signature pieces a part of my home and cabin and move them from room to room to keep the look fresh, satisfying my perpetual need for change in a continual quest to create new vignettes, new tablescapes, and always, new homes.

A signature piece doesn't have to be expensive. You can get the look without the seventeenth-century armoire. Painted furniture is really beautiful, so in vogue, and often quite reasonable in comparison to pricey antiques. The key is finding a piece you really love and want to live with forever.

Color is important in making that first impression in a home's living areas. A red living room can be just as inviting as a neutral color such as soft blue, gray, cream or sand. It's all about the way you use color that makes the difference between a room that is jarring and one that is comfortable to look at and be in. Using color smartly can also enhance your stellar display piece.

A Louis XV table in my library is covered with antique velvet. A Staffordshire figural lamp takes center stage on the table. The matching walnut bergères are Louis XV Revival style, circa 1930. A salt glaze cachepot adorns the table. The books surrounding the room give it warmth and personality. Tucked beneath the table is a German bronze Cavalier King Charles Spaniel, resting on a cushion.

In my small library, a room I always want to have in my home, a gate-leg center table is highlighted with a monumental vase on a stand. Illuminating the room is a tole Directoire chandelier, converted from its original life as an oil light. On the paneled wall and between matching swing-out lamps is a Scottish oil portrait of a child. This is one of the coziest rooms in my home.

Usually in public spaces, the dominant piece suggests how a room will be arranged. In French country homes, the hearth was typically the focal point of the main living area. In this country, too, a well-appointed fireplace mantel is often the focal point. Sometimes an armoire, an antique commode, or a painted reproduction sideboard can become the focal point around which the rest of the room is organized.

In a library or study, I like to use floor-to-ceiling bookcases brimming over. Books are like old friends: I feel comfortable surrounded by my favorites. Whether vintage or new, they create an inviting atmosphere and make a design statement all their own. My last house didn't have a library and I truly missed it.

When finished with favorite collections, art, mirrors, sconces, lots of decorative pillows, custom lamps and shades, and, always, fresh flowers, a home's public rooms come to life and enchant guests, as well as those who live there.

This room could easily be a fabled, period salon in Paris. The Haskins' formal living room, done in red and cream, presents a look of pure elegance and grace. A heraldic mirror above the sofa is flanked by gold brackets and Imari vases and sconces. Everything in this room is arranged symmetrically, with pairs of candlesticks, matching lamps and fresh flowers as accents.

Swedish painted cupboard in the family room is home to a collection of books, plates and flag figurines. Confit jars adorn the top of the cupboard. The custom chair on the right is upholstered in Rose Tarlow, and the fauteuil (armless chair) is "Sophie" from my custom furniture line. The slipper chairs are covered in Bennison fabric, and the draperies are Pierre Frey.

A painted commode in the Salisbury family room is host to several Staffordshire cow figures. The lamps are fashioned from wooden candlesticks. Watercolors by James Steinmeyer, plates with a nature theme, and an old lantern decorate the wall above the commode, and a miniature settee sits at the base. Striped side panels accent the French doors leading to the patio.

Tracy and I found the mantel and the antique botanical prints on a trip to France. The antique olive jar is sitting on a wood fragment that serves as a wall bracket. On the mantel between the antique faux bois jugs and candlesticks is a ceramic sculpture of a basket of mushrooms. Family portraits grace the coffee table.

The overall view of the Bakers' great room exudes wonderful charm. Above the cast-stone mantel by James Kelley is an original oil painting by Leonard Wren, who is known for his beautiful landscapes, including those of the French countryside. The sofa is covered with a Brunschwig & Fils check fabric. The wing chair is "Sophie," from my custom furniture line and is covered in toile by Pierre Frey. The floor-to-ceiling bookcases reveal a beautiful collection of blue-and-white Chinese export porcelain, which is very compatible with all the touches of red in the room.

Lee Jofa's "Tree of Life" fabric set the stage for the design in the Salisbury library. The custom rug repeats all the colors in the drapery fabric. Of special interest is the purple horsehair, metal-studded Regency bench arranged by the painted barley twist table. Also of note is the antique red chinoiserie desk, which picks up the red in the Lee Jofa fabric.

FAR RIGHT
Beautiful beading trims this elegant lamp in the Salisbury library.

LEFT

Behind closed doors, the inside of the shelves and facing are lined with a striped fabric and trimmed with a pretty braid instead of the more traditional gimp. The television is housed in this piece of furniture.

RIGHT

The "Tree of Life" Lee Jofa fabric in the Salisbury library was also used to upholster this antique chair.

FACING

A custom banquet-style sofa is in a niche all its own, surrounded by floor-to-ceiling bookcases revealing the Salisbury family's love of reading. The small oil painting is by Tulsa artist Wendy Matson.

LEFT

Proof that contemporary and traditional can live together harmoniously is seen in the gracious living room of Carol Pielsticker's contemporary home, the only contemporary home I've ever done. The stone mantel and overmantel are beautifully decorated and include tole urns with porcelain bouquets found at the Paris Flea Market. The sofa is covered in Coraggio fabric; the chinoiserie coffee table is by Rose Tarlow. A modernistic painting by Tulsa artist Otto Decker blends well with the sleek architectural style of the home.

ABOVE

An antique French stone mantel in the Salisbury living room is highlighted with an elegant trumeau mirror, lavishly draped with dried leaves and silk ribbons. Pewter pots hold dried hydrangeas, and a stone figure holds a stone bouquet. A child's settee rests in front of the fireplace. Miniature chairs and sofas add interest to a design and seem especially right in a home where children are growing up.

A Louis XIV commode in the entry of
Sharon and John Baker's home is flanked by
antique Louis XI carved-walnut side chairs
covered in Bennison fabric. The lamps are
from Vaughan, with custom shades, and are
a pretty complement to the magnificent
antique chinoiserie-style English foot bath.
Above the commode is an original oil painting by Leonard Wren.

Quiet, muted colors, beautifully textured fabrics and fabulous antiques make this a special room in the Baker home. The French Country buffet displays a prized collection of tortoiseshell. The duo of chairs on either side of the sofa are "Patrice," from my custom furniture line. Brunschwig & Fils chenille fabric graces the sofa. A Bennison oak leaf– pattern fabric covers a pair of chairs and is used in the side-panel draperies dressing the arched windows.

Regency side chairs and a striped ottoman add warmth to the entry scene in the home of Patti and David Bowman. On the antique English Adams-style console is a collection of Italian polychrome and gilt wood candlesticks. A pair of Portuguese Vista Alegre vases rest on bronze ormolu putti (cherubs) on both sides of the Regency gilt wood mirror.

A simple buffet, probably originally at home in a French chateau kitchen, belonged to me two homes ago, but I sold it because it was too large for later homes. As I so often do with antiques I love, I bought it back when a client wanted something fancier. Now it's perfect for the entryway in my new Tulsa home. A pair of nineteenth-century Directoire side chairs accent the buffet. The large painting was originally four inches taller, but I cut off the base of it to accommodate space in a previous home. A symmetrical collection of transfer and Chinese export plates are companions to the landscape painting. A Swedish painted clock, which has enjoyed different settings in numerous homes, is to the right of the buffet.

LEFT

The Haskins' sunroom is elegant in shades of soft yellow, gold and blue, but very comfortable and easy to entertain in. Side panels were the perfect choice to dress the windows without obscuring the lovely view of their back lawn. Tole chandeliers add muted lighting to this room, where Staffordshire figures star in several vignettes. Liz Haskins says, "When the sun comes up it just fills the room with light. It's rather spiritual. Our cats love to sun bathe in here."

BELOW

This intimate setting in the Haskins' sunroom invites spirited conversation. It is one of their favorite places to entertain and is conveniently adjacent to the dining room and kitchen. An antique oriental rug anchors this space. "This is where we talk about everything," says John. "This is the room where everything happens."

This view of my living room shows my fondness for symmetry in the arrangement of chairs that flank the fireplace and chairs placed near the windows, giving a view of the home's east landscaping.

RIGHT

A pair of Louis XV walnut bergères a la reine, circa 1750, flank the fireplace in the formal living room in my Tulsa home. The over-mantel of carved wood includes a small painting of Nicholas by Tulsa artist Janet Davies. The mantel is accented with Delft lidded jars, a Louis XV equestrian trophy ormolu mantel clock and a pair of quite rare Napoleon II dog candlesticks, purchased on my first visit to the Newark Fair in Nottinghamshire twenty years ago. Near the mantel are a Chinese export garden seat, a jardiniere and an ottoman upholstered in a leopard print.

The sitting room off my kitchen houses my collection of Staffordshire cows in the bookcases and on the mantel. Above the mantel hangs a country painted trumeau with an Empire-style tole chandelier. Nicholas enjoys the antique Country French wing chair covered in Pierre Frey fabric.

The luxurious entry in the home of Michael and Dru Hammer has a variety of unusual focal points. A pair of French fauteuils and a French fruitwood game table set the tone for the beauty to come in the rest of the home, which was originally built for musician Henry Mancini. A large fruitwood breakfront, circa 1860, a beautiful oriental rug and a Spanish-style chandelier are other accents. A "faux" butler stands beside the impressive painting Twelve Butterflies, painted by Donald Sultan in 1996.

Art from some of the nation's best master artists is the dominant theme in this area of the Hammers' living room. An eighteenth-century commode creates an elegant setting surrounded by magnificent art. Above the commode is a painting, Les Boutons S'ouvrent, by Marthe Orant. On the easel is a small painting, Sally Fairchild, by John Singer Sargent. On the right is Me'ne et Enfant, by William Bouguereau.

The arched doorway leading to the back lawn adds a distinctive architectural touch to the Hammer home.

LEFT AND BELOW

The spacious living room of the Hammer home blends an interesting mix of furnishings, art and accessories. The ceiling is accented with unusual wood beams. Dru Hammer's passion for hot pink and green is reflected in the color combinations of prints and stripes. The antique French limestone mantel is highlighted with a large painting by Donald Sultan. To the left of Sultan's contemporary painting is a drawing by Henri Matisse. A nineteenth-century Persian rug pulls the colors in the room together.

A duet of French chairs, sconces and antique French engravings create a beautiful setting in Julie and John Nickel's living room. The Louis XVI-style "Corbet Lounge" chairs by Minton Speidell are upholstered in Old World Weavers "Carlotta Diamond." An antique French side table rests between the chairs. The drapery swags and cascades have an underlay jabot and side panels made of silk by Old World Weavers with custom fringe. They are mounted on custom gold rods and finials.

RIGHT
Comfortable elegance characterizes the formal living room in the Nickel home. A beautiful crystal chandelier lights the room, showing off the numerous touches of graceful design. Sofas by George Cameron Nash are upholstered in Travers "Melo" and accented with custom pillows. A pair of "Warwick" cocktail tables by Minton Spidell have a custom finish; they are anchored in front of the fireplace, facing a pair of French wing chairs upholstered in "Marquis," a Scalamandré fabric. The tufted ottoman is upholstered in a coordinating Old World Weavers fabric, and the custom rug with an Antoinette border was designed by Edward Fields. The fireplace mantel holds antique candelabra, accented by an Impressionistic oil painting by Leonard Wren.

The Minton Speidell "Medici" sofa, with its carved and gilded accents, is upholstered in "Bellagio" by Fabricut, with custom silk pillows. Two antique French commodes with matching lamps and sconces flank the sofa. A pair of antique French fauteuil chairs are upholstered in Old World Weavers' "Florian Stripe." The portrait above the sofa, titled Children of the Reverend William Mussage Bradford, *was* painted by William Thomas and was exhibited at the Royal Academy in London in 1812.

FAR LEFT
A pair of marble-and-ormolu lamps with custom shades highlight the antique French commodes by the sofa. A crystal-and-silver caddy holds fresh flowers. The porcelain foxglove was made by Jimmy Nichols.

LEFT

Because my Spring Creek friends like to work jigsaw puzzles, I added the little card room addition in the living room to accommodate this happy pastime at the cabin. The table is an antique metal-top work-table and the side chairs are antique Swedish Montgolfier design.

RIGHT, TOP

I painted the original knotty pine paneling off-white for a lighter look in the cabin's living room. The pair of chairs on the right are reproduction "Sophie" chairs from my custom furniture line. The Rose Cummings fabric for those chairs was pivotal to the look I wanted to achieve. The sofa, "Roxanna," is in my custom line and the fabric is Brunschwig and Fils. Above the sofa is an antique chinoiserie clock, accented by a grouping of oil paintings, all by the same artist and found together at the Paris Flea Market. The custom lamps fashioned from antique Chinese soy jugs also have custom shades.

RIGHT, BOTTOM

The commode in the living room is a painted repro-duction. The antique birdcage is from Keith Skeels in London. The painting above the commode is one of my favorites—a child's portrait from the Louis XV period, purchased at Hotel Drouot in Paris.

A cozy den adjacent to the Renberg-Silberkleit kitchen is a perfect place for relaxing. The room expresses a lovely mix of patterns and color, especially Nancy's favorite color, green. A large bergère chair is upholstered in an embroidered linen floral fabric by Chelsea. The dark green sofa is dressed with custom pillows. An Asian chop table sits close to a miniature French child's chair. Masie Lee, the dog, is equally at home in this room and the living room.

The living room in the Renberg-Silberkleit home is a study in gracious formality. The limestone mantel hosts a tortoise-shell box with antique bronze dore candlesticks. A David Hockney painting hangs above the mantel. Antique French wing chairs nestle up to the fireplace. By the sofa, a pair of Barbara Barry–designed chairs are covered in gold-and-crimson cut velvet. Nancy's King Charles Spaniel, Masie Lee, is quite at home in this room.

FAR LEFT
Sleek and chic best describes this Lucite-and-glass game table in the living room. The Austrian Biedermeier chairs fashioned of silver birch and ebony are upholstered in olive-green-and-metallic-gold silk and velvet. A contemporary glass sculpture shares table space with vases of fresh flowers by Eric Buterbaugh. A chinoiserie box and an antique bronze watch holder complete the tableau. The large silk screen is by Larry Bell.

One of Nancy Renberg's favorite collections is tortoise-shell. A silver wishbone that is actually a sugar tong rests on one of the tortoiseshell boxes. The antique tole tray was inserted to become part of the large coffee table. The fresh floral arrangement was designed by Eric Buterbaugh.

An Austrian Biedermeier burled elm bibliothèque, circa 1820, serves as a beautiful transition piece from the living room into an arched hallway. The painting in the hallway is by Peter Max.

The dramatic entryway in the Los Angeles home of Nancy Renberg and Jack Silberkleit features an unusual patterned wallpaper, an antique French umbrella stand and a photo realism painting of a waiter by Tulsa artist Otto Duecker.

RIGHT

A Louis XV fruitwood country buffet has an eye-catching presence in the Herndon entryway, with a pair of Regency-style side chairs framing the vignette. A Chinese lacquer sewing box is among treasures accenting the buffet.

FAR RIGHT

A mix of antiques and contemporary touches are seen in this vignette on the fruitwood country buffet. A custom lamp was made from a vintage tole urn, accented by a small old-world painting. Fresh peonies add a touch of spring in a stylish, contemporary, heavy glass vase.

FACING

A pair of Louis XVI bergère oreilles serve as excellent companions to a Louis XV provincial cherry table de ferme, hosting a custom lamp, a small painting, a pair of candlesticks, an English Regency tea caddy and a cachepot filled with fresh flowers, designed by Toni Garner of Tulsa.

RIGHT, TOP

A Minton Speidell low table is the central focus in the Herndon living room, surrounded by the Louis XV/XVI bergères and a sofa. Matching English Regency girandoles add luster to the walls.

RIGHT, BOTTOM

A pair of Louis XV–XVI transitional bergère chairs frame the fireplace in the living room of Amy Herndon's home. The mantel features a Victorian gilt bronze sculpture representing autumn. Chinese export vases hold floral arrangements also designed by Toni Garner. Carvings accent both sides of the mantel for a look that displays my love for symmetry.

FACING

A long hallway leading from the entryway is decorated with an antique ribbon-
backed Chippendale settee and an
antique French bibliothèque. One of the
Hammers' treasures in this hallway is
an oil portrait of Michael's grandfather,
Dr. Armand Hammer, painted by Marc
Kleonsky in 1990.

BELOW

A glass-top table in the Hammers' long
hallway has an antique French iron base.
Partially shown is a lithograph titled
Prayer Meeting, by George Bellows.

This comfortable and eye-appealing sitting area off the Hammers' kitchen is dressed in a blue-and-white color scheme. The antique French Country sofa is inviting. A custom pewter lamp highlights an end table. The family cat, Mr. Big, is quite comfy in this room.

A wrought-iron chandelier presides over the second entry-way to the Hearst home. A Spanish table stars in the center of the room, holding an Italian bookstand, Italian altar sticks, and a santos.

Books, art, and family portraits make a distinctive backdrop in the Hearst home for a vignette that includes an antique horn chair, a small table with a custom Staffordshire lamp, and an antique Louis Vuitton steamer trunk that now serves as a coffee table. A leopard-print rug ties this room together.

FACING

The view from the fireplace in the Hearst home reveals a custom-made coffee table featuring an unusual antique needlepoint top. An antique gilded mirror rests above the French commode. The beautiful side panels fronting the French doors are trimmed with striped silk and lavish fringe in shades of blue and brown. Art fills the walls in this beautiful and comfortable living room.

ABOVE

The Louis XV walnut mantel in Joanne Hearst's home is elegantly dressed with a nineteenth-century animalier oil painting, a precious find of a favorite artist at an antiques fair in Avignon. A pair of English-style club chairs are companions to a duet of Directoire-style painted bibliothèques.

ABOVE

In the entry of Joanne Hearst's finca in Spain, a magnificent Brittany Henri II sideboard is a showpiece. It is highlighted by Italian altar sticks and a painting of the Patron Saint of Seville, Santa Justa, and the old Moorish part of the cathedral tower. The side chairs by the buffet are upholstered in reproduction fabric from the Hearst Castle in San Simeon, California.

A pair of French bonnetières flank the fireplace in the inglenook, and an antique Spanish trunk serves as the coffee table. A French pastry table holds a pair of lamps and a collection of Portuguese bovines. The upholstery on the matching side chairs reflects Joanne's fascination for horses and carriages. A pair of horses and a large contemporary painting of a horse accent the mantel.

Soft beige and neutral colors make Joe and Priscilla Tate's living room a restful and relaxing setting for living and entertaining. A pair of French bergères flank the sofa, which has a subtle fleur-de-lis pattern. One of the pair of French wing chairs by Yale Berge is upholstered in Fortuny fabric. A pair of antique French chairs in their original fabric once belonged to Priscilla's mother and add interest to the small French commode. The curtains are lush striped silk and feature beautiful fringe. Simple rods and gold rings are the finishing touches for the side panels.

LEFT

An iron-and-glass coffee table in the Tate formal living room is accented with a beautiful tablescape, including a pair of silver candlesticks, a silver compote and two vases—one a slender rectangle filled with hydrangeas and the other with fresh tulips, designed by Toni Garner. Books, Imari plates and a handsome magnifying glass complete the vignette. Boomer, one of the Tates' Welsh Terriers, enjoys this view from his perch in one of the French bergère chairs.

entertaining spaces

*les espaces
de détente*

WHETHER I'M ENTERTAINING casually in the kitchen, setting a formal table in my dining room, or hosting friends al fresco on the patio, I find the most important thing is for my guests to be comfortable and have fun. I want them to enjoy this special occasion, and even if it's a formal gathering, I like to approach entertaining with a sense of humor.

Often the style of a dining table dictates how formal or informal the occasion will be. A country kitchen with a harvest table suggests more casual affairs, while a Louis XV reproduction table and chairs call for a dressier, more formal event.

While I love casual suppers, I also like formal entertaining in my dining room at home in Tulsa. All you really need for successful entertaining is fresh flowers, 40-watt light bulbs in the chandelier, and the ambience of candlelight. How could you miss?

The formal dining room of the Hearst home is fitted out with Sevillano painted furniture created by a local artist, who decorated the chairs with birds, flowers, garlands of berries and a flower-filled urn. The stone reproduction mantel features elegant candelabra and fruit bowls of flowers framing a French mantel clock. Antique French sconces accent the walls.

A canary named Ricky Martin is always a guest at my formal dinner parties in the dining room, and he sings his head off. His elaborate birdcage was a housewarming gift, so when I moved into a new home, Ricky had a beautiful new home, too. My grandmother always had a canary and I remembered that from my childhood. This is my third or fourth bird, and the canary always chirps happily away, as if on cue, while I entertain.

With beautiful silver, crystal, china and linen napkins, a table set in fine style looks gracious and welcoming without being intimidating.

RIGHT

A painted antique cupboard to the left of the open shelving holds everyday glassware and dishes, making them easily accessible for spur-of-the-moment entertaining.

FACING

I love open shelving in a kitchen because it is very much a hallmark of French kitchens. I especially like open shelving in a country setting. It seems more informal and casual and complements the kind of easy entertaining I like to do at the cabin. More antique pewter tankards are featured on these shelves.

FACING

A pine farm table, circa 1870, serves as the dining table in my cabin, "The Roost," on Spring Creek, in northeastern Oklahoma. A pair of antique rooster candelabra accents the table. The pivotal piece in the room is a Country French painted sideboard. I decorated it with an antique birdcage, antique tole bouquets, pewter tankards on brackets with a pewter plate over the birdcage. It's no secret that I love chickens, so I especially like the custom lamps I had fashioned from heirloom Staffordshire chickens. The grape-stake fencing between the beams on the ceiling add unusual textural interest.

LEFT

A French-style tole chandelier lights up the breakfast area in the Herndon kitchen. Louis XV dining side chairs are a pretty accent around the small, footed table. Side panels of brown-and-white check with wood tassel fringe frame the paned windows.

Dru Hammer found this set of French chairs in the attic of an antiques shop and thought they were worth restoring, even though they were in total disrepair. Now they are beautiful, fully restored, surrounding the round dining table, over which light from a Baccarat chandelier casts a warm glow. Hanging above an antique French buffet is a French trumeau. The painting above the fireplace is by Vincenzo Migiaro (1850–1938). To the right of the door is a painting by S. Pascal. In the hallway is a photo realism painting of Armie and Victor Hammer by Tulsa artist Otto Duecker. The flowers in this setting are by Eric Buterbaugh, of Los Angeles.

A magnificent oval table is the centerpiece of the Hearst dining room. A
quartet of silver candlesticks and fresh
flowers in a silver repoussé bowl set an
elegant table. Antique plates and framed
antique silverware decorate the wall, and
the tole chandelier adds drama to the
setting. Above the mantel is a portrait
of Joanne's granddaughter.

In the Bakers' great room, which also serves as
the breakfast area, all the furnishings are cozily
arranged to face the fireplace. The antique French
fruitwood table is surrounded by Country French
side chairs circa 1860, and above the table hangs
a reproduction red tole chandelier. Red tole lamps
on the antique pine dresser base accent a horn
mirror and Staffordshire cows. Toile curtains dress
the windows.

A lovely accessory at the Bakers' French fruitwood table is a copy of an eighteenth-century
banquette a deux, dressed with Pierre Deux
plaid cushions and toile pillows.

Reproduction Windsor chairs circle the English gate-leg dining table—also a reproduction—in the Bakers' dining area. The host chairs are from my custom furniture line and are covered in a Brunschwig & Fils cotton check that is repeated on the sofa pillows. The collection of antique majolica and pewter are elegantly displayed on the nineteenth-century oak dresser from South Wales.

An Italianesque faux-marble-and-wrought-iron table serves me well in my formal dining room. I used Directoire-style dining side chairs, and they comfortably seat eight guests. Above the table is an eighteenth-century Italian chandelier that has been in just about every home I've owned. In the background is a treasured birdcage.

A large painting by Frank Stella serves as a dramatic focal point in the Renberg-Silberkleit formal dining room. The iron-and-glass dining table was made by Dale Gillman, of Tulsa's Antique Warehouse. The chandelier was designed by Niermann Weeks. Paintings on the side walls are by the Dutch-born American painter Willem de Kooning.

The round dining table in the Tate home is fashioned of Carpathian elm. The unusual pie-shaped leaves extend to seat twelve guests. The dining room chairs are antiques from Kentshire Gallery, New York. The elegant crystal chandelier is the perfect accent for the antique footbath holding a fresh flower arrangement by Toni Garner. The dining room draperies are in my favorite style: side panels with a single swag and a cascade of Scalamandré silk. The sideboard, dressed with a pair of custom lamps and Imari plates, is centered by an ornate footbath. The painting is by French artist Charles Camoin.

In the Herndon dining room, a massive Louis XV oak center table serves as the dining table, lighted by an Italian painted chandelier. A Louis XV provincial enfilade is accented by a stately mirror and accessorized with a pair of nineteenth-century tole floral altar sprays on brackets and a pair of English Regency–style zinc jardinières. On the dining table, two large hurricane lamps frame a floral arrangement in Japanese lacquer and bronze brazier.

RIGHT

A French sideboard is the stage for a pair of custom lamps and a wall treatment that showcases the Tuckers' beautiful collection of Minton Florentine china, which was an heirloom gift to Francesanne and John from his great-grandmother. The lamps feature shades fashioned of Fortuny fabric. A porcelain foxglove was made by Jimmy Nichols of Paducah, Kentucky. Beautifully carved French chairs accent the sideboard.

FACING

Formal elegance is evident in the dining room of Francesanne and John Tucker, of Tulsa. Custom side panels and a graceful swag in Fortuny coral fabric, with sheer cafés, drape the bay windows. A French tiered server is used as a buffet for dinner parties. A bronze sculpture of two game birds is a focal point on the top tier of the table. The dining table is centered with a pair of antique silver candlesticks and an Imari footbath with a floral arrangement of hydrangeas and white and coral tulips by Tulsa florist Toni Garner.

private spaces

les espaces privés

SOME OF THE MOST special rooms in a home are those private spaces, bedrooms and baths and dressing rooms. Color is the key to creating a space that will inspire relaxation and I think the color palette should be quiet, calming and restful, suggesting the feeling of a retreat away from the cares of the day.

Because we usually begin and end our days in a bed, a bedroom should be especially beautiful, comforting and relaxing—a place that truly soothes the soul. I also believe the bathroom and dressing room deserve as much attention to beauty and detail as the rest of the home.

For me, the attention to detail begins in the dressing room. Organization brings me a great deal of comfort, and I've always had a fondness for well-organized closets and dressing rooms. Places where clothing is hung or folded neatly in place, easy to see and ready to wear makes life so much simpler and gets the day

RIGHT

The bed in the master suite of Tina and Elby Beal's home is magnificently dressed with a coverlet in a floral and bird theme. The lit a baldaquin—a canopy bed—features three complementary fabrics. The pillows of checks with accents of the coverlet fabric are trimmed with ornate fringe, braid and petite silk balls.

off to a better start. And there's no reason that these most private of spaces can't be pretty as well. Even when rooms seem to be overflowing with shelves of books, patterned walls, heirloom collectibles, comfortable overstuffed sofas and chairs, I gravitate to orderly, symmetrical arrangements with a focal point. That is really very much the way French homes look. By imposing order with balanced arrangements, one can insert beautiful objects and still not overpower a room.

I like to use furniture, usually antiques, rather than built-ins for dressing rooms and closets. Antiques have so much more charm and give these private spaces a personality all their own. I usually include a chair, a commode, books, paintings, and framed photographs of family and friends that will bring memories of special times together. I decorate a closet or dressing room just as I would any other room in the house.

The bedroom in my own home now features the bed that was in the guest room in my last house. The color palette is subtle, like the soft beige palette used throughout the home; previously, though, I had a red bedroom and found it restful and warm. (I don't recommend red for children's rooms, as the stimulating color seems to make them hyper.) My clients, family and friends all know red is my most favorite color, and I don't think I could live without it. I've created many red rooms, often without using red paint, as fabrics, wallpapers and upholstery are great ways to make a red room.

CENTER

The lit close in my cabin is ever so tiny, but red-and-white toile—one of my all-time favorite fabrics—used in various patterns throughout the room makes a grand statement for guests. Space is at a premium in most of the Spring Creek cabins, where mine is located; this room was actually created from two closets and was serving as the laundry room when I purchased the cabin. Since I don't know how to use a washer and dryer, I put the space to better use. The enclosed high box bed—the lit close—is surrounded on two sides by bookshelves. The coverlet is an antique French quilted picnic cloth. The antique Swedish chair has an antique paisley throw. The antique table was carved to resemble a tree trunk.

It's interesting to note that bedrooms were uncommon in French country homes in the nineteenth century. People either slept by the fire in the salle (living room) or in lofts. If a family was lucky enough to have a bed, it was often draped for privacy not only while sleeping but for getting dressed.

Draping the bed is one of the hallmarks of Country French design, whether the drapery fabric is a gossamer sheer, yards of silk that puddle on the floor, an ambient storytelling toile, or any of the beautiful florals that give a bed a touch of forever springtime. When a room lends itself to that kind of sensuous, romantic draping, I enjoy adorning the bed with beautiful fabrics and luxurious trims.

Perhaps the most important accessory in my bedroom at my Tulsa home is the small step chair that Nicholas uses to reach the bed. My brother-in-law, Dale Gillman, makes the step chairs for my clients from little chairs and upholsters them in fabrics that complement the room's color theme and decor.

A red-and-cream floral paper decorates the Beals' master bathroom walls. An antique marble-topped chest is home to the lavatory, which is accented with a companion chair covered in blue-and-ivory toile. A large three-sided ottoman—Sophie the dog's favorite resting place—is covered in a blue-and-white Bennison fabric, and trimmed, rather ornately, with soft blue fringe.

I used one of my favorite wallpapers in the bathroom, the squirrel and scroll pattern with oak leaves and acorns by Osborne and Little. It makes a wonderful backdrop and I've even used it in the entryway for some of my clients. An antique marble-topped commode was fashioned into a vanity in my quest to often give new uses to old furnishings. A Black Forest carved match holder and vase holds miniature sunflowers.

LOWER RIGHT

A canine theme definitely prevails in the bathroom at my cabin. I have collected dog portraits for years and find them whimsical and heartwarming in this setting.

FACING

An eighteenth-century Provincial fruitwood armoire is the signature piece in the cabin's bathroom. But the beautiful antique French arched window, draped by side panels, and the eighteenth-century French enamel and metal tub with twenty-first-century fittings also vie for attention. Above the tub, a Black Forest carved bracket holds a dog, antique miniature papier mâché horn trophies and another dog painting. A comfy antique chair is a perfect place to put towels for guests.

I found this French antique faux-bamboo bed, circa 1860, at the Paris Flea Market and fell in love with it. I created the bed niche by building a pair of closets to frame the bed. The ceiling features an antique tole chandelier, and above the bed are antique, hand-colored bird engravings. The drapery fabric is a Brunschwig & Fils paisley. The table at the end of the bed, which began life as an antique leather gun case, is now supported on a brass frame. The walls and ceiling were clad in rough cedar and then white-washed for a rustic look, just perfect for the cabin.

FACING

A small Louis XVI love seat anchors the cozy, romantic space in the Pielsticker sitting room. A brass and marble Directoire table faces a fauteil chair covered in silk by Duncan Ticking. The wall covering is by Zoffany. Exquisite fabric by Brunschwig & Fils drapes the windows. The heavy fringe adds another layer of richness to the small room.

BELOW, LEFT

A towering painted circa-1880 French bibliothèque that was found at the Paris Flea Market presides over the Pielsticker sitting room. Although it was too large for the space, cutting two inches off the top and bottom made it a perfect fit

BELOW, RIGHT

A contemporary glass-topped metal desk by Niermann Weeks is a handsome complement to the Frank Lloyd Wright–style windows in Carol Pielsticker's small home office, where she handles family and community correspondence.

I restyled Carol Pielsticker's dressing room, which originally had all of the storage built in. Now, an antique French desk serves as her dressing table. It is attired elegantly with a pair of tole lamps from Vaughan, providing a clean, symmetrical look. The subtle wall covering is by Rose Tarlow. The small window got star treatment with a swag and a cascade in striped silk.

A side chair with a bamboo look has its original needlepoint fabric. This chair in the Pielsticker dressing room, adjacent to the master bedroom, makes a perfect companion to the French-style chair at the dressing table.

A santos figure seems quite at home on a silver tray on Pielsticker's dressing table. Antique jars and glass boxes hold makeup brushes, cotton tufts and other toiletries.

An antique chest was converted to twin lavatories in the master bathroom of Melissa and Scot Ison. An ornate Venetian mirror rests against a larger mirror and is accented by twin sconces. Blue-and-white check side panels frame the window, with half sheers added for privacy.

BELOW LEFT

A Swedish chest found at the Paris Flea Market makes a beautiful accessory in the Isons' master bedroom. Matching lamps and tole floral arrangements dress the top of the chest, which is accented with a decorative tassel. A pair of French chairs flanking the fireplace are covered in "Nadette" woven lisere in spring green by Brunschwig & Fils.

BELOW RIGHT

Staffordshire figures, an antique plate, a basket of ivy and a lovely arrangement of hydrangeas and greenery adorn the French garden table in the Isons' master bedroom.

FACING

An antique writing desk and a chaise lounge, purchased in France, provides a cozy place for reading, relaxing and writing letters in the Isons' master bedroom.

CENTER

The Isons' bedroom is truly a rhapsody in blue. Yards of voluminous cotton and silk in hues of pale blue and ivory frame the bed. We mixed some reasonably priced fabrics with others that were lush and more expensive and splurged on the elegant fringe to trim the draperies and pillows. To the right of the bed, an antique French garden table is handsome in its new use as a night table.

FAR LEFT

Striped silk taffeta trimmed with blue-and-white check encircles the Isons' bed. The fabric for the coverlet, curtains and chairs is "Inga," in oyster, by Waverly. A paisley throw adds to the pleasing mix.

CENTER

The bath in the Haskins' master suite is a testimony to flowers and ribbons, a springtime theme that delights Liz every time she enters the suite. The beautiful wallpaper is "La Drapery" by Scalamandré. An antique French buffet converted to a lavatory features a pink marble top accented by two ornate gilt mirrors. Antique fashion prints decorate the walls.

FAR RIGHT

In the Haskins' master bath, the sink, hand painted by Wantha Ann Deaton, of Tulsa, repeats the wallpaper motif of ribbons and flowers. The custom hardware is by Sherle Wagner.

I believe every home needs a red room, and the study of Dr. John Haskins demanded to be painted red. This is a masculine atelier, with lots of books, Napoleonic memorabilia, and a grand desk that anchors the small room.

This tiny space, tucked between two facing closets, is a real show stopper on the upstairs landing leading to the Haskins' guest suite. The French daybed, with its cane sides, is elegantly dressed in a richly textured raspberry upholstery and lavished with custom pillows. Pink-and-lime silk draperies and a valance—all trimmed with lavish fringe—add interest to the window, which leads to an outdoor balcony. Yummy, the Haskins' Red Persian cat, likes to nap here.

FACING

An antique chest got a new lease on life when converted to a lavatory in the Haskins' guest suite bathroom. One of the elegant touches in this room is the antique mirror (at right), hung from a decorative ribbon. Plush towels, small-frame paintings, and an airy floral arrangement create a welcoming look to this guest bath.

FACING

The Haskins' guest bedroom truly expresses a feminine spirit. The beautiful brown carpet with pink floral design blends well with the toile. The bed skirt puddles to the floor, giving the bed dressings a rich look. Liz says guests are very comfortable in these quarters, which also feature an adjacent dressing room and bath.

ABOVE

The Haskins' guest bedroom is a wonderful study in brown-and-white toile; it covers the walls and adorns the feminine French chairs that sit on either side of the ornate antique desk. Toile drapery side panels, accented with my trademark fringe, dress the windows. Yummy loves to nap under this desk, too

FACING

In the Nickels' home, the custom vanity by Kerns-Wilcheck is finished with a marble top. The vanity stool by George Cameron Nash is upholstered in "Falk Manor House" by Scalamandré and has custom trim by George Cameron Nash. The wallpaper in soft colors of cream, pink and green is "Revillon" by Zoffany.

The formal living room in my home is dressed in quiet colors—neutral beige for the sofa and chair upholstery and for the side panels draping the windows. Above the sofa is a Louis XVI gilt wood barometer, accenting a black-and-white engraving of a Napoleonic battle scene. A painted cast-iron-and-glass low table, an old favorite of mine, is nestled between the sofa and chic modern slipper chairs, a la designer Billy Baldwin.

ABOVE

Faudree master bedroom. The eighteenth-century Italian commode—accented by a Regency
bull's-eye mirror, framed engravings and brackets with Napoleonic figures—was the entry
piece in my former home. Decorating is truly a
moveable feast for me. The lamp is the first one
I bought when I graduated from college.
Nicholas's portrait has a place of honor on the
commode, which also hosts my collection of
bronze dogs of all breeds.

The powder room has a regal look about it and is dressed in Dru Hammer's favorite color theme of hot pink and green. An antique chinoiserie mirror provides depth in the room. A pair of antique French bergère chairs and a small, antique, hot pink French settee accompany a small Italian commode. A leopard-print carpet is a contrast to the hot-pink-and-green-striped fabric in the side panel draperies and the green-and-white frog wallpaper. This is definitely a room that expresses my philosophy that "it's the mix, not the match."

An antique French stove was innovatively transformed into a lavatory in the Herndon powder room. A vintage repoussé mirror makes a beautiful decorative statement. An oriental bowl is cleverly used for the lavatory.

Using a cutout of the bench fabric gives this decorative pillow, framed in elegant fringe, more depth on the Swedish bench.

Embroidered bed panels by Chelsea House envelope the master bed. This is a favorite napping place for Polo and Beau, Golden Labrador Retrievers. A painted Directoire cupboard, circa 1860, houses a collection of treasured books, while the basket atop the cupboard holds magnolia leaves. An antique Swedish bench covered in Bennison fabric is a pretty addition to the room. The wing chair is by Niermann Weeks, upholstered in Ralph Lauren fabric. The coverlet features Manuel Canovas; the wall covering is Zoffany; and the silk check is Travers. The bedside commodes are antique Provincial furnishings.

Wisteria wallpaper by Nina Campbell makes the perfect backdrop for Nancy Rinberg's dressing room and bath. An antique French chandelier from the Paris Flea Market lights the room. A Louis XVI Provincial mirror is a contrast to the Emilio Terry–inspired 1940's mirrored dressing table. The elegant draperies are fashioned of "Sonti" lavender silk stripe by Stroheim & Romann.

An antique French metal wall ornament is fashioned into a pretty towel rack that displays some of Nancy Renberg's collection of antique linens.

An antique iron safe topped with marble became the sink and vanity in the guest bathroom. The architectural motif in the wallpaper is "Garden Pavilions" by Zoffany; it's the same wallpaper I used in the guest bathroom in my own home in Tulsa.

RIGHT

Pale lavender and moss green present tranquil, restful hues in the master suite in the Renberg-Silberkleit home. The bed and bed dressings are by Ann Gish. A Louis XV commode at the right is accented by a Peter Max painting. The chairs in the foreground are Louis XVI armchairs covered in "Chantemerle" by Pierre Frey.

Pale lavender-and-cream-striped wallpaper creates a pretty background for a collection of antique clocks that hang in Nancy Renberg's closet.

RIGHT

Wallpaper by Rose Tarlow is the back-drop for this subtle treatment in the master bathroom of the Tucker home. The custom-built vanity was painted by Tulsa artist Bob Phillips. An antique painted slipper chair is upholstered in Fortuny fabric. The wall decor above the chair features room renderings by New York artist Jim Steinmeyer.

A pair of porcelain lovebirds accents the
vanity in the Tucker bathroom. Also shown
on a silver engraved tray is part of a collection of unusual snuff bottles.

One of the eight guest rooms in the Hearst home features an antique French iron bed draped with embroidered linen side panels. The quilted coverlet and mix of fringed floral-and-checked pillows creates a soft, soothing combination. The draperies and valance of blue-and-yellow toile add a cheerfulness to this lovely room.

Joanne's pretty bedroom is very feminine, with a perpetual display of primroses, tulips, and other flowers from an English garden. The antique French tole bed is beautifully painted with even more flowers, and the canopy is attired in a floral print that matches the draperies and makes an unusual space for a bracket displaying a carved-wood santo. Floral paintings accent the walls in this pastel paradise of yellow, green and lavender, and dark wooden beams accent the ceiling. Rika, one of Joanne's dogs, takes a nap in a floral upholstered wing chair.

A lovely collection of pillows decorates Joanne's bedroom. The mix of checks and florals results in a stunning combination.

outdoor
spaces

les pièces en extérieur

THE FRENCH LOVE THE OUTDOORS and find delight in each region's distinctive style. Much of the charm of their homes is found in the way flowers burst out of colorful window boxes, shrubs and trellises dress properties small and large, and ivy drapes a boldly painted home. Their fascination with dining in the midst of nature is legendary, too.

France's American counterparts like to observe nature from garden rooms and three-sided rooms. For seasonal outdoor entertaining, I love garden rooms and indoor/outdoor rooms that open to a view of nature. They are fun to decorate and so easy to entertain in. I think the trick is to let nature dictate the design of these spaces and to use colors, fabrics and elements that look like they belong in a lush garden setting.

Nothing defines an outdoor space or garden room better than wicker and rattan, and boxcar siding is wonderful for walls in these areas. Stone flooring or scored concrete is not only practical but can be beautiful with just the right glaze. Canvas and denim, florals and pillow ticking are always

In the west garden room in the Salisbury home are a variety of textures to please the eye, from wicker to stone. Shells and antique botanical prints add to the nature theme expressed in the decor.

congenial companions in spaces that transition from inside to outside. Beamed ceilings add to the comfortable spirit I like to create.

Other natural accessories such as seashells suggest a perennial seaside nostalgia and enhance the outdoor garden theme. Or, framed antique botanical prints can make a statement in a garden or outdoor room, especially when grouped together for impact.

One of my favorite decorating ploys in rooms with an outdoor or garden theme is to display antique garden implements in an old grape carrier hung on a wall. They add a rustic, almost whimsical, look. I've used this theme in my own homes several times as well as in homes of clients.

Outdoor rooms are perfect for furnishings that have a hearty look, such as stone or iron coffee tables and planters. Folding tables and folding French chairs add to the ambience, easily accommodating drop-by guests. Antique stone urns are right at home here too, filled with vibrant, seasonal flowers or plants.

I also love when these spaces have a fireplace with a welcoming hearth, a staple in a French Country home. With the warming flames and wonderful scent of a wood-burning fire, these special outdoor rooms can become at-home retreats, even on chilly autumn or early spring evenings.

Garden rooms and outdoor rooms are a wonderful way to court nature and enjoy its bounty within the comfort of a room with a view.

FACING

The centerpiece of the Bakers' outdoor room is a dry stack chimney adorned with an antique Republic of France flag holder. Comfortable furnishings and a sisal rug create a wonderful place to enjoy nature's theater—in complete comfort no matter what the weather.

BELOW

A wrought-iron staircase connects the east garden room to the children's playroom. Tracy bought the stairs and the folding table between the two chairs at the Paris Flea Market on one of our recent shopping trips.

An ivy topiary tree in the Salisburys'
west garden room shares a wall with a
collection of antique garden implements in
an old grape carrier, a decorating theme
influenced by London designer Kenneth
Turner.

FACING

Stone craftsman James Kelley, of Tulsa,
designed the reproduction mantel of cast
stone for the Salisburys' west garden
room. Iron urns filled with tole bromeliads
and a basket of shells adorn the mantel.
The mirror is framed in wicker; matching
wicker chairs are by Ralph Lauren.

Tulsa artist James Kelley designed the reproduction cast-stone fireplace in the Salisburys' east garden room. The mantel is accented with a pair of antique stone finials and a stone trough filled with ivy and ferns. Above the mantel is an antique pewter stencil pattern. A Country French armoire from the Paris Flea Market conceals the television.

ABOVE

Beau, one of the Salisburys' Labrador Retrievers, checks out the east garden room.

RIGHT

An old pine table in the east garden room provides a perfect view of the facing master bedroom. A pair of antique French folding chairs with leather strapping was found at the Paris Flea Market. The reproduction French chairs, "Sophie," are from my custom furniture line. Portieres filter the light in this sun-filled room.

The outdoor living spaces at the Renberg-Silberkleit home are decorated as beautifully as the interiors. With new iron garden furnishings, there is now plenty of space for the couple to enjoy gracious entertaining. The pillow fabric is a shell pattern by Scalamandré. The table is set with Nancy's French Faience tureen and bowls. They have a wonderful skyline view of Century City.

An antique iron fountain is the focal point in the entry garden at the Hearst home. Iron tables and floral-covered upholstery on the chairs make this a lovely place to greet guests, read a book or just enjoy the beauty of nature. Orange trees add a fragrant note to the garden. The home, designed by architect Hanibal Gonzales, was built in 1926. Gonzales also designed the Plaza de Espana and the Hotel Alfonso in Seville.

Lime green and hot pink on a black
background dress the outdoor room at
the Hammer home. We chose a mix of
florals, stripes and solid fuchsia to add
bold and inviting color to this area of the
home.

FAR RIGHT
Ziggy, the Hammers' Maltese, is the
most important accessory.

OVERLEAF
The great outdoors truly comes to life at
the home of Dru and Michael Hammer
in Los Angeles. In one of my favorite
three-sided rooms, we have created an
oasis here for relaxation. With sunlight
drifting in through the wisteria, the
seasonal look of this garden room is a
pleasing blend with the natural elements
just beyond the patio.

Wisteria is a beautiful focal point in the vista from the Hammers' garden room. Its vibrant purple blooms complement the color scheme of lime green, hot pink and black.

One of the terraces at Hearst's finca is furnished with iron furniture and decorated with black-and-white-striped cushions and pillows of Manuel Canovas' "Doria Roses." A large glass-and-iron coffee table makes this a grand setting for outdoor entertaining, especially when the wrought-iron sconces create soft candlelight for evening dining. Large columns add a dramatic look to this outdoor room.

Under the protection of a porch that is covered yet privy to maximum air circulation, this is truly a luxurious outdoor room, as sophisticated and comfortable as any room indoors.

finishing touches

les finitions

What canary wouldn't sing like a lark if she called this birdcage home? This is my canary, Ricky Martin. The elegant Loire Valley chateau-style birdcage was a gift to me from Tracy Lorton when I moved into my new home. Ricky sings at every dinner party, letting me know that he likes his new home. The birdcage rests on a wrought-iron patisserie table base.

Displaying collections is about balance and fooling the eye with different levels and wall groupings. Notice how the various levels let the eye rest periodically. This collection of dishes is a mixture of different colors of blue, from delft and blue transferware to English and Chinese export porcelain.

Details are like frosting on the cake. Sometimes people tend to stop before the job is done. Left, the pillows on are finished with a combination of fringe, braid and welt. Mixing materials also adds interest. On the bed (center) is a mix of cotton and silk. Pillows can dress up any bed or change the look of any sofa. They're magic in the way they transform a room. Notice also the fringe on the Tuscan lamp shade.

Accessories are as important to a room as the furniture itself. What makes the composition appealing in both of these groupings are the different eye levels and subject matter. In the grouping above, objects and materials are duplicated on each side of the center, creating the wonderful symmetry I love. On the right is an interesting arrangement of materials and dissimilar objects in an asymmetrical grouping. Both vignettes have fresh flowers—always a wonderful touch.

Acknowledgments

r e m e r c i e m e n t s

I thought I only had one book in me, but here we are again, and I am immensely grateful to everyone who helped me with this second one. I extend my sincere appreciation to the following:

The homeowners, who were so willing to allow us into their homes and lives to photograph their beautiful surroundings. They are Sharon and John Baker, Tina and Elby Beal, Patti and David Bowman, Dru and Michael Hammer, Liz and John Haskins, Joanne Hearst, Amy and Blake Herndon, Melissa and Scott Ison, Julie and John Nickel, Carol Pielsticker, Nancy Renberg and Jack Silberkleit, Tracy and Hal Salisbury, Francesanne and John Tucker, and Priscilla and Joe Tate. Merci.

Jenifer Jordan, whose incredible talent and hard work, created the beautiful photography in this book.

Nancy E. Ingram, photo stylist, whose talented eye and dedication set the highest standard for both of my books from beginning to end. She has been my wonderful friend for many years.

M. J. Van Deventer, writer and childhood friend, who had the job of cleaning up and organizing my rambling sentences and translating my thoughts on French Country design.

My staff and assistants for their time and support, and especially April Moore, who helped me create these beautiful homes.

Toni Garner and Eric Buterbaugh, talented and gifted floral designers who added the beauty of fresh flowers to the Tulsa and Los Angeles photographs.

Dale Gillman for giving freely of his time and for his vast knowledge of French provincial furniture.

Karl Engle, who made the job in Spain possible and an even greater joy.

Madge Baird, Gibbs Smith editor, for her commitment and enthusiasm, and who through the process has become my friend and for whom I have great respect.

Mary Ellen Thompson, for her design and attention to detail.

Most affectionately, my sister, Francie Faudree, for her constant love and support.

And to all of you, I cannot thank you enough.

Fondly,

Charles

Antiques and Resources

Références

CALIFORNIA

Ann Dennis
2915 Red Hill Ave
Suite B106
Costa Mesa, CA 92626
Phone: (714) 708-2555

Jefferies Ltd.
852 Production Pl
Newport Beach, CA 92663
Phone: (949) 642-4154

Kathleen Stewart At Home
338 North LaBrea Ave
Los Angeles, CA 90036
Phone: (323) 931-6676

Lyman Drake Antiques
2901 S. Harbor Blvd
Santa Ana, CA 92704
Phone: (714) 979-2811

Terra Cotta
11922 San Vicente Blvd
Los Angeles, CA 90049
Phone: (310) 826-7878

Tom Stansbury Antiques
466 Old Newport Blvd
Newport Beach, CA 92663
Phone: (949) 642-1272

Uniquities the Consignment House
and Uniquities Antique Mart
11740 San Vicente Blvd
Los Angeles, CA 90049
Phone: (310) 442-7655

Eric Buterbaugh Flower Design
300 S Doheny Dr
Los Angeles, CA 90048
Phone: (310) 247-7120

Villa Melrose
6061 W 3rd St
Los Angeles, CA 90036
Phone: (323) 934-8130

GEORGIA

Boxwood Gardens & Gifts Inc.
1002 E Andrews
Atlanta, GA 30305
Phone: (404) 233-3400

The French Attic The Stalls
116 Bennett St NW
Atlanta, GA 30309
Phone: (404) 352-4430

Jane Marsden Antiques
2300 Peachtree Rd NW
Atlanta, GA 30309
Phone: (404) 355-1288

NEW YORK

Elliot Galleries
155 East 79th St
New York, NY 10021
Phone: (212) 861-2222

George N. Antiques
67 East 11th Street
New York, NY 10003
Phone: (212) 505-5599

Herbert De' Forge
220 E. 60th St
New York, NY 10022
Phone: (212) 223-9007

John Rossellie
523 East 73rd St
New York, NY
Phone: (212) 772-2137

King Antiques
57 East 11th St
New York, NY 10003
Phone: (212) 253-6000
        (212) 674-2620

Royal Antiques
60 East 11th St
New York, NY 10003
Phone: (212) 533-6390

NORTH CAROLINA

Ryan & Company
384 Hwy 107 S
Cashiers, NC 28717
Phone: (828) 743-3612

The Country Home
5162 US Hwy 64 East
Highlands, NC 28741
Phone: (828) 526-9038

Rusticks
32 Canoe Pt
Cashiers, NC 28717
Phone: (828) 743-3172

Vivianne Metzger Antiques
31 Canoe Pt
Cashiers, NC 28717
Phone: (828) 743-0642

OKLAHOMA

Antique Warehouse
Dale Gillman
2406 E 12th St
Tulsa, OK 74104
Phone: (918) 592-2900

Cisar Holt
1609 E 15th St
Tulsa, OK 74120
Phone: (918) 582-3080

Royce Meyers Gallery
1706 S Boston
Tulsa, OK 74119
Phone: (918) 582-0288

Sam Spacek
8212 E 41st St
Tulsa, Ok 74145
Phone: (918) 627-3021

S.R. Hughes
3410 S Peoria
Tulsa, OK 74105
Phone: (918) 742-5515

T. A. Lorton
1345 E 15th St
Tulsa, OK 74120
Phone: (918) 743-1600

The Antiquary
1323 E 15th St
Tulsa, OK 74120
Phone: (918) 582-2897

Colonial Antiques
1740 S Harvard
Tulsa, OK 74112
Phone: (918) 743-6700

Kelley's Antiques
8202 E 41st
Tulsa, OK 74145
Phone: (918) 282-2045

Polo-Lodge Antiques
8250 E 41st
Tulsa, OK 74145
Phone: (918) 622-3227

Robert's Antiques
168 E 15th St
Tulsa, OK 74120
Phone: (918) 582-1058

Toni's Flowers & Gifts
3525 S Harvard
Tulsa, OK 74135
Phone: (918) 742-9027

Arthur Graham
7118 N Western Ave
Oklahoma City, OK 73116
Phone: (405) 843-4431

Covington Antique Market
7100 N Western Ave
Oklahoma City, OK 73116
Phone: (405) 842-3030

TENNESSEE

A Little English
4554 Poplar Ave
Memphis, TN 38117
Phone: (901) 682-2205

Catherine Harris
2115 Merchants Row
Germantown, TN 38138
Phone: (901) 753-0999

TEXAS

Country French Antiques
1428 Slocum St
Dallas, TX 75207
Phone: (214) 747-4700

George Cameron Nash
150 Dallas Design Center
1025 N Stemmons Freeway
Dallas, TX 75207
Phone: (214) 744-1544

Joseph Minton
1410 Slocum St
Dallas, TX 75207
Phone: (214) 744-3111

The Mews
1708 Market Center
Dallas, TX 75207
Phone: (214) 748-9070

Pierre Deux
415 Decorative Center
Dallas, TX 75207
Phone: (214) 749-7775

Uncommon Market
2701 Fairmont
Dallas, TX 75201
Phone: (214) 744-3111

The Whimsey Shop
1444 Oak Lawn Ave
Dallas, TX 75207
Phone: (214) 745-1800

Area
5600 Kirby Dr
Houston, TX 77005
Phone: (713) 668-1668

Brian Stinger
2031 West Alabama
Houston, TX 77098
Phone: (713) 526-7380

Joyce Horn Antiques
1008 Wirt Rd
Houston, TX 77055
Phone: (713) 688-0507

Kay O'Toole Antiques &
Eccentricities
1921 Westheimer Rd
Houston, TX 77098
Phone: (713) 523-1921

PARIS

Paris Flea Market
Marche Aux Puces
Saint-Ouen Flea Market
Porte De Clignancourt